Understanding My Emotions

When I'm Embarrassed

Understanding My Emotions

When I'm Angry
When I'm Embarrassed
When I'm Happy
When I'm Lonely
When I'm Overwhelmed
When I'm Sad
When I'm Scared
When I'm Sorry
When I'm Surprised
When I'm Worried

Understanding My Emotions

When I'm Embarrassed

ALEXANDRA DALTON

**Understanding My Emotions
When I'm Embarrassed**

Copyright © 2016 by Village Earth Press, a division of Harding House Publishing. All rights reserved. No part of this publication may be reproduced or transmitted in any form or by any means, electronic or mechanical, including photocopying, recording, taping, or any information storage and retrieval system, without permission from the publisher.

Village Earth Press
Vestal, New York 13850
www.villageearthpress.com

First Printing
9 8 7 6 5 4 3 2 1

Series ISBN (paperback): 978-1-62524-440-6
ISBN (paperback): 978-1-62524-377-5
ebook ISBN: 978-1-62524-133-7
   Library of Congress Control Number: 2014944101

Author: Dalton, Alexandra.

Contents

To the Teacher or Parent	7
When I'm Embarrassed	8
Find Out More	42
Feeling Words	44
Index	46
Picture Credits	47
About the Author	48

To the Teacher or Parent

More than a hundred years ago, John Dewey insisted that the true purpose of schooling was not simply to teach children a trade but to train them in deeper habits of mind. Social-emotional learning builds on Dewey's theory further, suggesting that emotional skills are crucial to both academic performance and future success in life.

The research is definitive: emotional training is good for children! A recent study, reported in the *New York Times*, found that preschoolers who had even a single year of social-emotional training continued to perform better two years after they left the program; they were less aggressive and less anxious than children who hadn't participated in the program. Another study found that K-12 students who received some form of emotional instruction scored an average of 11 percentile points higher on standardized achievement tests. A similar study found a nearly 20 percent decrease in students' violent behaviors.

The goal of this series of books, UNDERSTANDING MY EMOTIONS, is to instill in young children a foundation of emotional intelligence. Use these books to help children learn to understand, identify, and regulate their emotions. Give them important tools that will serve them well for the rest of their lives!

When I'm

Embarrassed

I feel all sorts of things. Some of my feelings are fun to feel. Some aren't fun at all. When I do something stupid, I get a feeling that isn't fun!

When my stomach feels hungry, if I eat something that feeling will go away. The taste of an apple in my mouth is another feeling!

But if I eat TOO much, my tummy could start to hurt. That's a feeling too.

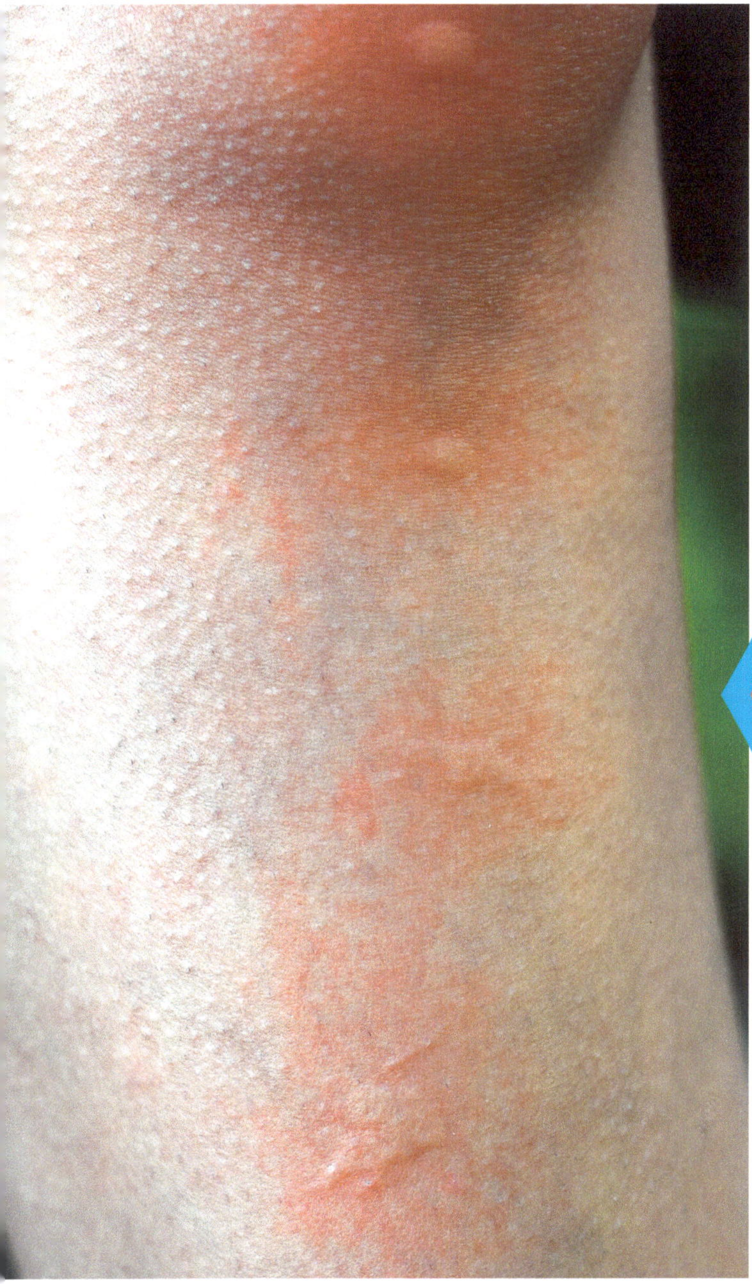

I feel itchy when I get a mosquito bite.

My throat feels sore when I have a cold.

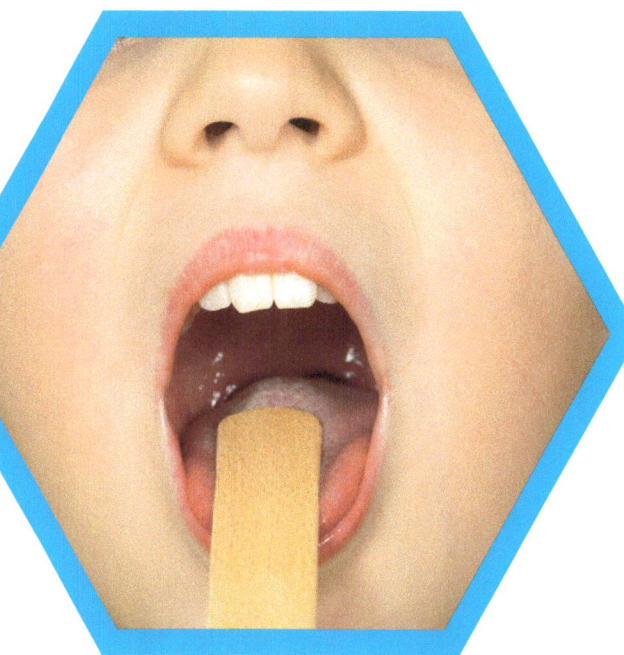

Those are all different things my body feels. But I have other feelings too. These feelings are called emotions.

Emotions come from my body too, just like my other feelings. Emotions mostly come from the part of my body called my brain. My brain is inside my head. It's wrinkly and kind of funny looking— but it does amazing things! It gets the messages from my eyes and ears, my skin, and my nose and tongue. It collects information from the world around me. Then it sorts out all that information. It decides what my body should do next. It's like the boss of my whole body.

My brain is busy all the time. It's the part of me that remembers. It learns new things. It helps me read.

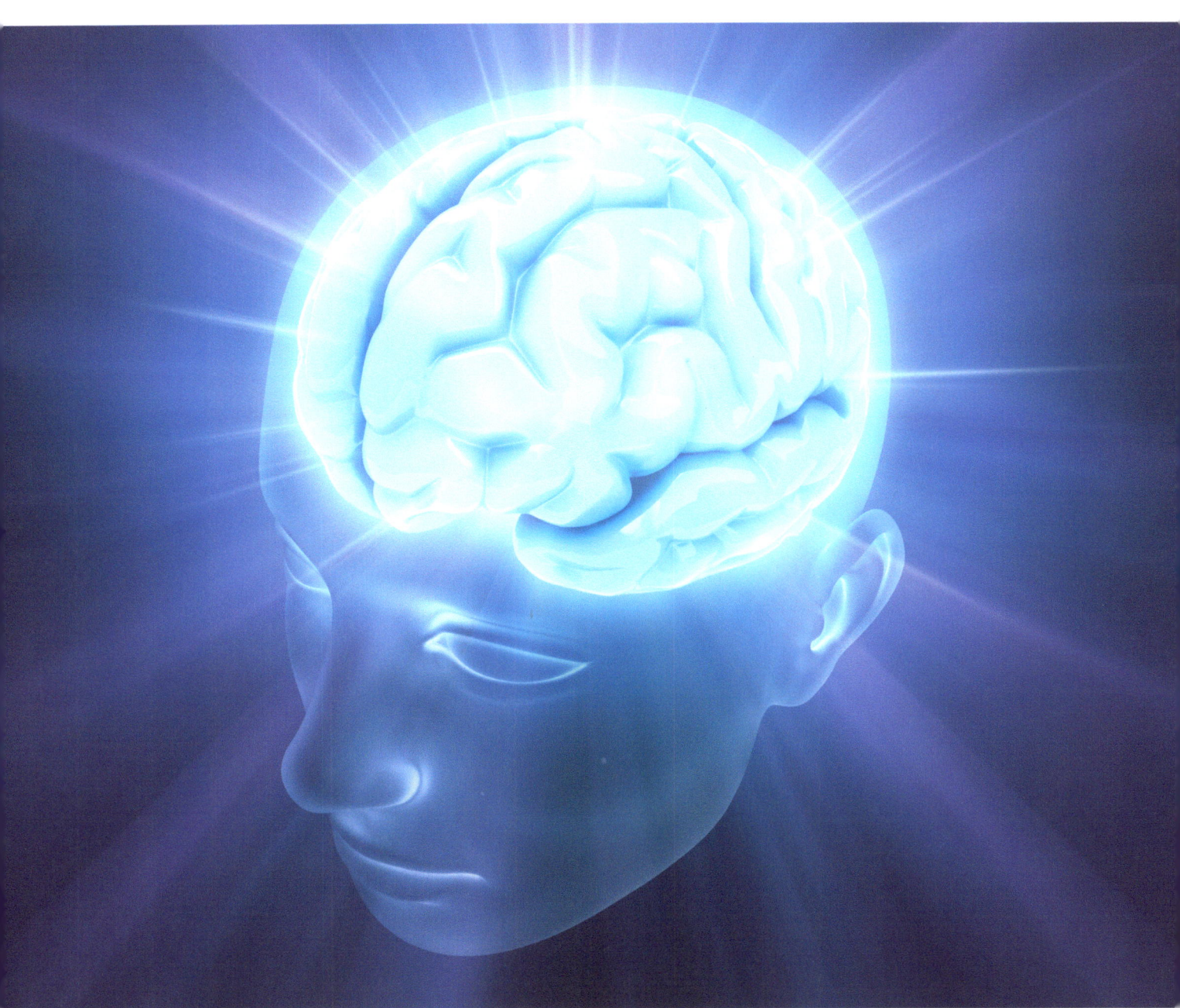

It tells my arms and legs when to move.

It comes up with lots of new ideas every day.

It controls pretty much everything that happens inside my body—my heart beating, my lungs breathing, and my food getting digested.

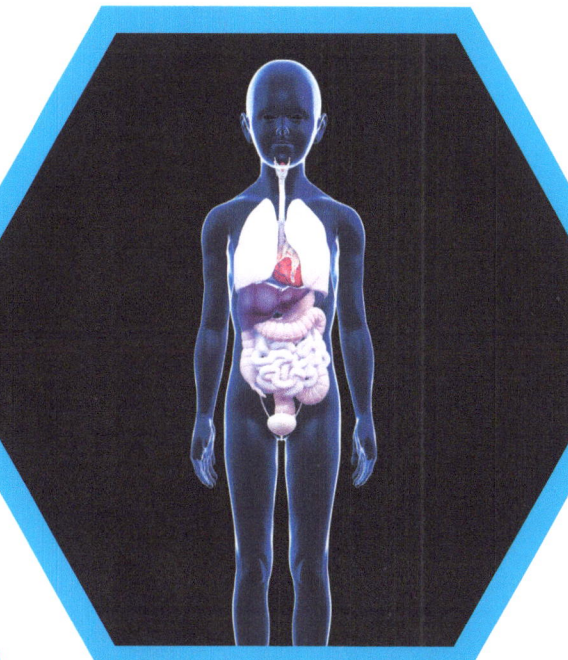

And my brain makes the feelings that are called emotions.

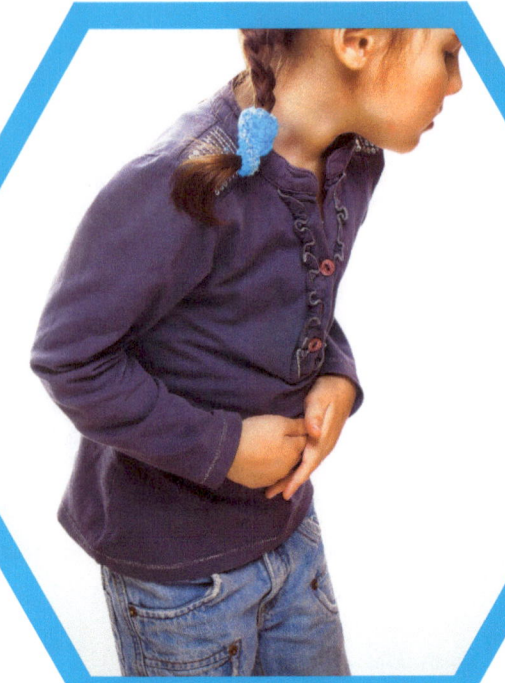

Even though emotions start out in my brain, they can make other feelings all over my body.

Emotions can make my stomach feel funny.

They can give me a headache.

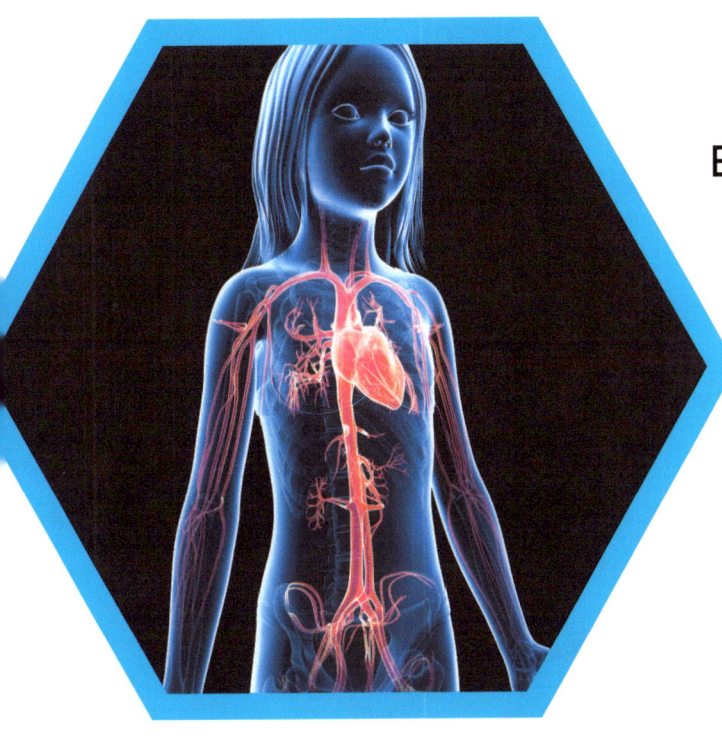

Emotions can make my heart beat faster. When that happens, more blood moves through my body.

Emotions can even make my hands sweaty!

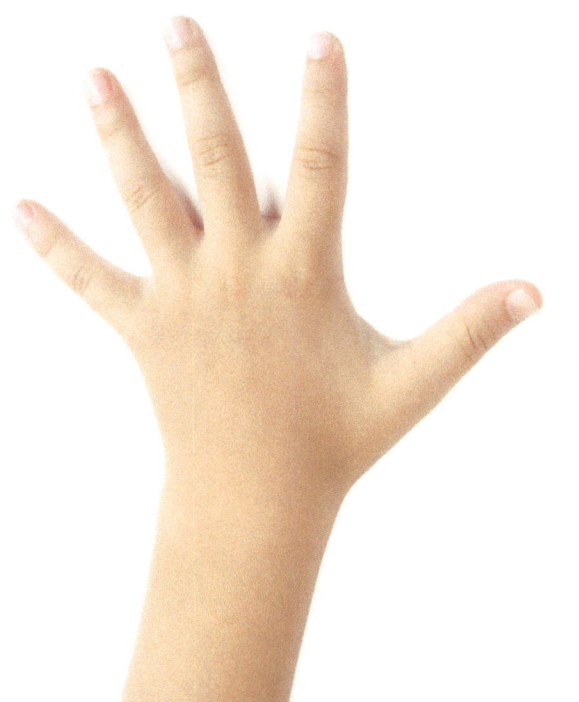

I have all kinds of emotions.

I feel happy when someone makes me laugh.

I feel angry when my big brother picks on me.

I feel excited when I listen to my favorite music.

When my goldfish died, I felt sad.

I feel frustrated when I forget my sneakers on gym days.

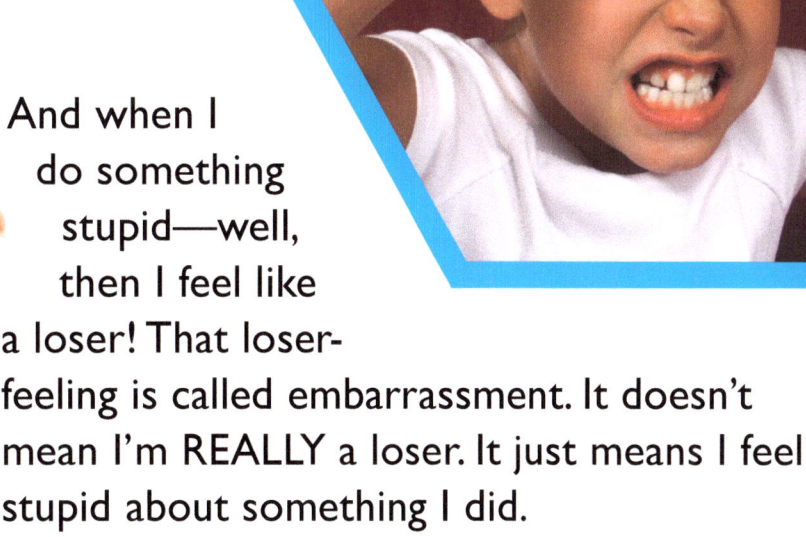

And when I do something stupid—well, then I feel like a loser! That loser-feeling is called embarrassment. It doesn't mean I'm REALLY a loser. It just means I feel stupid about something I did.

Embarrassment doesn't feel good. When I'm embarrassed, I feel as though I've done something wrong. It feels as though everyone is looking at me—but not in a good way! I'm afraid people are thinking I'm stupid. I feel silly and a little scared and shy, all at the same time.

    Sometimes I try to laugh it off—but inside I'm not laughing. My face turns red. I try to hide my face. I wish I could run away somewhere no one would see me!

Everyone feels embarrassed sometimes.

My friend Amanda feels embarrassed when she gets a bad grade at school.

Jason is embarrassed when the teacher asks him to do a math problem on the board. He hasn't done anything stupid—but he's afraid he might! He feels like everyone is looking at him. He thinks the whole class will laugh if he makes a mistake.

Nathan is embarrassed if he misses the ball when he's playing softball with his friends.

Lucy gets embarrassed at parties. Everyone else is having fun—but she doesn't know how to join in. She's afraid the other girls will think she's a loser!

Even grownups get embarrassed!

My mom says she feels embarrassed when she makes a mistake at work.

My Uncle Tony gets embarrassed when we tease him about his new girlfriend.

My dad is embarrassed when people tell him he's going bald!

My grandpa feels embarrassed when he forgets to do something.

Embarrassment isn't fun! I HATE it when I feel embarrassed. But I don't have to feel like a loser!

Even if I make mistakes, I can still feel good about myself! I can still like being me.

There are things I can do to help me handle embarrassment. The first thing I can do is call this feeling by its name. When I know the names of my emotions, I understand myself better. I know why I feel the way I do. I don't have to give up or get really upset when everything seems horrible. Instead, I remember that feelings come from my brain—and they don't usually last very long.

When I feel really stupid about something I did, I say to myself, "I'm not stupid. I'm just embarrassed." I know that embarrassment is just an emotion that comes and goes inside me. Everyone in the whole world feels embarrassed sometimes!

When my friends are better at something than I am, I remind myself that there are plenty of things I AM good at. I'm not very good at softball—but I don't have to feel embarrassed about it. I'm really good at music. I can't be good at everything!

Sometimes I feel embarrassed because I'm scared of things that don't bother my friends. I don't know how to swim very well because I'm so frightened. I'm scared of jumping in the water. But I don't have to feel like a loser because swimming scares me. There are other things that scare my friends that don't scare me. My friends are really scared of my pet snake—but I'm not scared of him at all!

Feeling embarrassed can make me afraid to try things that I'm not good at. I feel embarrassed every time I go to the pool with my friends, because they're not afraid and I am. But I don't have to let embarrassment be the boss.

Even though I can't play softball very well now, I can get better at it. The more I practice, the better I get. Maybe I won't ever be as good as some of my friends—but I can still have fun. I don't need to let embarrassment hold me back!

I can learn not to feel as scared at the pool. The more I practice getting in the water, the less scared I feel. I still feel a little embarrassed when I don't dare jump in the pool with a big splash, like my friends do. That's okay. Every time I get in the pool, my embarrassed feelings get smaller and smaller. Instead of being embarrassed, I feel proud. I'm proud because I've learned to do something that scared me!

Feeling embarrassed can make me want to hide. I don't want anyone to look at me. I feel sad inside. I pull away from my friends and my family. I tell people to leave me alone.

But when I feel embarrassed, sometimes the best thing to do is laugh. Laughing lets people know I'm not going to let embarrassment be my boss. Nothing seems as bad when you laugh!

Sometimes my body embarrasses me. One time I burped while I was talking to my babysitter. I felt so embarrassed! Another time, I sneezed and snot sprayed all over my friends. They all shouted, "Gross!" and I felt my face turn red with embarrassment. And I felt REALLY embarrassed the time I farted during class and everyone heard me. I just wanted to crawl under a rock and hide!

But everyone burps, even my babysitter.

Everyone has sneezed sometime without a tissue to catch it.

And absolutely everyone in the whole world farts. My dad farts, my mom farts, all my teachers fart. Even the president of the United States farts!

When I farted in class, everyone giggled. But they didn't think I was a stupid person, even though I felt like they did. They've all farted too! Kids just think farts are funny.

People with good manners try not to burp or fart in public. They try to sneeze into a tissue. But we can't always control our bodies. When a burp, a big sneeze, or a fart slips out, we just need to say, "Excuse me!" Maybe we laugh it off. It's just not a big deal.

Kids even pee their pants at school once in a while, which is really embarrassing for them. But that's another thing we all do—we all pee. Even my dog has accidents sometimes!

The time I got sick at school, I was so embarrassed when I threw up all over my desk. No one wants to throw up, especially not at school—but everyone gets sick sometimes. Even grownups. Sometimes we just can't help what our bodies do.

My friends aren't trying to be mean when they laugh at something I did. They don't know I feel embarrassed. I try to laugh with them, but sometimes I just can't. It's okay for me to let my friends know how I feel. I can say, "Please don't laugh at me. Don't tease me. I already feel embarrassed. When you laugh at me and tease me, I feel worse."

When I pay attention, I notice when my friends feel embarrassed too. When that happens, I can let them know I don't think they're stupid. I can tell them it's not a big deal. I can let them know I still like them just as much as ever. I can make sure I don't tease them.

Everybody does things that make them feel embarrassed. The next time YOU feel like you've done something stupid, don't let embarrassment be the boss! Here are some things you can do:

- Remember that embarrassment is just a feeling in your brain. It doesn't mean you're REALLY stupid. It's just an emotion, and the feeling will go away.

- Laugh it off.

- If you can't laugh right now, remind yourself that whatever seems so awful right now could seem really funny next week or next month.

- Tell yourself, "It's not a big deal." Then get busy and move on. Don't think about it anymore.

- Remember—everyone does stupid things sometimes. Sometimes the reason people laugh is BECAUSE they've done the very same thing you just did.

- If your embarrassment doesn't go away and you can't stop thinking about it, tell a grownup you trust. You should feel good about being you. If you're feeling embarrassed day after day, ask for help.

Most of all, remember— you are NOT a loser!

Find Out More

You can learn more about your emotions by going online and checking out these websites. Some of the sites have videos you can watch or games you can play. You could also read the other books in this series to find out more about feelings—or you could go to your library and see if you can find the books listed on the next page. There's a lot more you can learn about worry and other feelings!

On the Internet

It's My Life: Emotions
pbskids.org/itsmylife/emotions

KidsHealth: Feelings
kidshealth.org/kid/feeling

Model Me: Faces and Emotions
www.modelmekids.com/emotions_dvd.html

In Books

Burns, Ellen Flanagan. *Nobody's Perfect.* Washington, DC: Magination, 2008.

Cook, Julia. *Tease Monster.* Boys Town, NE: Boys Town Press, 2011.

Dismondy, Maria. *Spaghetti in a Hot Dog Bun: Having the Courage to Be Who You Are.* Portland, OR: Bookbaby, 2011.

Espeland, Pamela. *Proud to Be You.* Minneapolis, MN: Free Spirit, 2006.

Lamia, Mary C. *Understanding Myself.* Washington, DC: Magination, 2010.

Moss, Wendy. *Being Me: A Kid's Guide to Building Confidence and Self-Esteem.* Washington, DC: Magination, 2010.

Pett, Mark. *The Girl Who Never Made Mistakes.* Chicago: Sourcebooks Jabberwocky, 2011.

Feeling Words

Feeling embarrassed is just one of our feelings. There are many other feelings, and many words we use to describe them. Here are some of them.

Proud

Scared

Shy

Sorry

Surprised

Bored

Index

An index is a way you can quickly find something inside a book. The numbers tell you exactly what page to turn to if you want to find that word.

angry 18

body 11–12, 15–17, 34, 36–37
brain 12, 15–16, 27, 40
burp 35–36

dad 25, 35

emotion 11–12, 15–18, 27, 40
excited 18

face 20, 34
family 32
fart 35–36
food 15
friends 22–23, 28–32, 34, 38–39

frustrated 19

good manners 36
grandpa 25

hand 17
happy 18
head 12
headache 16
heart 15, 17
hungry 10

itchy 11

laugh 18, 20, 22, 33, 36, 38, 40–41
loser 19, 23, 26, 29, 41
lungs 15

mistake 22, 24, 26
mom 24, 35
music 18, 28

parties 12, 23
pee 37
proud 31

sad 19, 32
school 22, 37
sick 37
sneeze 36
softball 23, 28, 30
stomach 10, 16
stupid 9, 19–20, 22, 27, 36, 39–41
swimming 29

tease 24, 38–39

Picture Credits

p. 8: © Rebecca Abell | Dreamstime.com

p. 9: © Rebecca Abell | Dreamstime.com

p. 10: © Rebecca Abell | Dreamstime.com, © Ulrich Willmünder | Dreamstime.com

p. 11: © Christi 180884 | Dreamstime.com, Ron Sumners © | Dreamstime.com

p. 12: © Rebecca Abell | Dreamstime.com

p. 13: © KTS | Dreamstime.com

p. 14: © Win Nondowkit | Dreamstime.com, © Rebecca Abell | Dreamstime.com

p. 15: © Sebastian Kaulitzki | Dreamstime.com, © Alan Lacroix | Dreamstime.com

p. 16: © Maxximm | Dreamstime.com, © Gvictoria | Dreamstime.com

p. 17: © Sebastian Kaulitzki | Dreamstime.com, © Riderofthestorm | Dreamstime.com

p. 18: © Rebecca Abell | Dreamstime.com (all images)

p. 19: © Dave Bredeson | Dreamstime.com, © Rebecca Abell | Dreamstime.com

p. 21: © Rebecca Abell | Dreamstime.com

p. 22: © Monkey Business Images © | Dreamstime.com, © Robert Kneschke | Dreamstime.com

p. 23: © Scott Griessel | Dreamstime.com, © Marcel Kroi | Dreamstime.com

p. 24: Leslie Banks © | Dreamstime.com, Athol Pady © | Dreamstime.com

p. 25: © Mauro Rodrigues | Dreamstime.com, © Atholpady | Dreamstime.com

p. 26: © Rebecca Abell | Dreamstime.com

p. 27: © Anna Szonn | Dreamstime.com

p. 28: © Rebecca Abell | Dreamstime.com

p. 29: © Rebecca Abell | Dreamstime.com

p. 30: © Serban Enache | Dreamstime.com, © Tony Dudley | Dreamstime.com

p. 31: © Rebecca Abell | Dreamstime.com

p. 32: © Rebecca Abell | Dreamstime.com

p. 33: © Rebecca Abell | Dreamstime.com

p. 34: © Rebecca Abell | Dreamstime.com

p. 35: © Stefano Lunardi | Dreamstime.com, © Scott Griessel | Dreamstime.com, © Atholpady | Dreamstime.com

p. 36: © Michael Zhang | Dreamstime.com

p. 37: © Mark Carper | Dreamstime.com, © Atholpady | Dreamstime.com

p. 38: © Feverpitched | Dreamstime.com

p. 39: © Calamity John | Dreamstime.com

p. 41: © Rebecca Abell | Dreamstime.com

p. 44: Fotolia: © Fasphotographic, © Cantor Pannato, © Andres Rodriguez, © Gabriel Blaj, © Moodboard Premium, © Halfpoint

p. 45: Fotolia: © Cantor Pannato, © Blend Images, © Zhekos, © Olly, © Wavebreak Media Micro; © Serrnovik | Dreamstime.com

About the Author

Alexandra Dalton was a teacher, and now she is a writer. When she was a teacher, she helped her students talk about their feelings. She knows that it's hard work sometimes to talk about our feelings—but she knows we feel better and we get along with each other better when we can use our words to talk about how we feel. Alexandra has three children. She also has a dog and a cat and four goats. She lives in New York State.

www.ingramcontent.com/pod-product-compliance
Lightning Source LLC
Chambersburg PA
CBHW061359090426
42743CB00002B/67